This book
Please read
return.

MW00945107
v

FROM DEATH TO LIFE

One Man's Journey Out of Addiction and into the Hands of God

DEDICATION

I'd like to start by honoring two people in my life who have not only sacrificed much to help me get to where I am but have also been the best parents possible. Without them, I don't know where I would be. Mom, Dad, I love you more than words can accurately express. You guys have done so much for me over the years; even through the pain, you continued to fight for my life. Thank you from the bottom of my heart.

From Death to Life

2018 © Bryson Layne Clark

All Rights Reserved. No part of this publication may be repro-
duced, stored in a retrieval system or transmitted in any form or
by any means – electronic, mechanical, photocopy, recording or
any other – except for brief quotations in printed reviews, without
the prior permission of the author.

To connect with Bryson:

soldier4Christ719@gmail.com

TABLE OF CONTENTS

INTRODUCTION

Addiction is a messed up trap of the devil. It is a trap he uses to keep people from becoming who God has created them to be, and he will do whatever it takes to keep them addicted. I found a solution one day to my problem with this demon called addiction. His name is Jesus!

In this book, I will be sharing the testimony of my life and how I was delivered from ten-year drug addiction. I almost died multiple times and was even pronounced legally dead at one point, but was miraculously brought back to life – and then I found a new life in Christ! I will be sharing with you some very hard times. Some of the details may be a bit drastic and graphic, but it's only to paint a picture of just how bad it was and how far God has truly brought me.

I'll be talking about all that took place in my life leading up to the time I started using drugs, the years while I was an addict and how I came to overcome addiction through the power of the blood of Jesus and the Holy Spirit. I will also be sharing the testimony of many things that took place after I surrendered my life to God including several encounters I've had with Him, miracles I've seen, and how God has used my life since then to share the love of Jesus all around the earth. And if He can do it for me, He can do it for anybody!

What is a testimony?

Testimony is a funny thing. The Israelites, who God calls his chosen people in the Bible, actually believed that the word **testimony** was more than just someone speaking out what God had done for them. They believed that "testimony" meant what God had done before he would "do again." Therefore, today, when someone shares a testimony of what God has done, it actually has the power to recreate that same testimony right there where it's being shared in the life of those hearing it. It then becomes a declaration that God will do again what He has already done in the life of another person. This is my hope for this book. As you read the testimony contained within these words, I hope that it will be more than an inspirational message or an encouraging book, but that as you read it, you will literally be brought into a deeper encounter with the heart of God. I pray particularly for those who find themselves in need of this same deliverance and restoration from addiction. I declare over you that what He has done for me He will **"Do again!"**

Thanks for reading,

Bryson Clark

Chapter 1

THE BEGINNING

If you've only known the man I am today, you may not realize that at one point in my life I was a very different person. The transformation that's taken place within me has changed everything about my life. It's true that when the Bible proclaims that Christ will make ALL things new, He truly does make all things new. My life is a living testimony to that fact. I no longer am who I once was and have at times even referred to my life in two parts; the old life and the new life. It was almost as if someone reached up and flipped a switch within me and everything then turned in the complete opposite direction of where I was headed before. That's what God does, right? When He gets ahold of someone, everything begins to change. The old has passed . . . Behold, the new has come!

Let's start at the beginning...

April 12, 1987. This is the day that I was born. Interestingly, this happened to be the same day in 1861 that the Civil War began. On the day I was born, another war – a spiritual one – began over my life. Reflecting on that day, my mom recalls that moments before I was born, while she was lying in her hospital bed, suddenly the monitors recording my heart beat stopped, alerting the staff that my heart had stopped beating. Nurses rushed in and turned her over, and my heart began to beat again. I believe that the enemy had it out for me since day one; that from the beginning he looked for ways to claim me as his own. I now know that God also had a plan for me. For years I would walk a much opposite path than what God had planned for me, but I've always belonged to Him no matter where my life would take me.

As a young boy I was pretty smart – in fact, when I was in third grade I was the smartest kid in my class, but I frequently got bored with the work. Over the years I developed the habit of simply "tuning out." I was even placed in all advanced classes because my ability in math and English was well beyond the other students who were in the same grade. Math particularly was my strong suit.

I've always had this way with numbers and seemed to be able to do very difficult math problems with little effort.

Every Sunday I went to church either with my parents or grandparents. Some Sundays we attended the Baptist church where I loved how they used instruments when they sang. Other times we attended services at the local Church of Christ. Though they never used musical instruments, the different levels of vocals and harmony drew me in. I usually sat in the pew, drawing and keeping quiet through the services so that I didn't cause a commotion during the singing and the preaching. I remember one pastor specifically more than the others. Murphy preached at the Church of Christ, and he was probably in his mid-40s. He had dark curly hair that was cut in a funny style – kind of like a mullet. I can still hear his voice to this day, but I can't remember a single specific thing he said. What I do remember is that he would speak through the microphone, and it would echo through the church so loudly that it seemed like the light fixtures in the chapel were going to fall.

More times than not, my five senses were tuned in to my surroundings. I was amused by the sound of the microphone echoing loudly, and I was preoccupied with the scent of the perfume on the woman who sat in front of us every Sunday. Sunday after Sunday the scent was the same. To this day I can still smell that sweet, fragrant aroma so well; it is almost as if I am smelling it at this very moment. As I look back now, another memory of my young church-going days is a particularly fond one. It is that my grandma always had fire- flavored Jolly Rancher candies on hand for me to eat. I waited all week for those fire- flavored candies, and I loved going to church with my grandparents mainly for the candies. Maybe God was filling me with the fire all along, I just didn't recognize it!

I attended church almost every Sunday as a young boy, but I still had no understanding of who Jesus really was. I didn't know about God as a father or that I could have His very Spirit living in me. As I look back, I realize that my memories of attending church as a young boy were limited to what I could only physically hear, smell, or touch. In my mind, church was a place to be entertained by the harmony of the music, the echo of the microphone, a preacher with a mullet and flavored Jolly Ranchers. My eyes had clearly not been opened to see, nor were my ears opened to hear the truth of God's Word.

My little sister, Kalli, was born when I was four years old in 1991. We were pretty close as kids, but later on, my drug addiction would put some unnecessary tension between us. My parents were always good to us, but we did not have a perfect family. My dad drank frequently, and he actually was the one who first introduced me to beer. Before I was even one year old, my dad would put beer in my bottle. I was a colicky baby, and he would put it in my bottle to calm me to sleep. He has since been completely freed of alcoholism by the mighty hand of God and carries quite a powerful testimony as well. Hopefully one day he will write that story himself. My mom never touched the stuff. She was the one who tried her best to keep us in line.

At the age of twelve, my family suffered an upsetting event which greatly affected me. My grandma, who we called Granna, who took me to church as a young boy had battled cancer from the time I was born, passed away. Granna was my dad's mom. At one point, early on in her disease, the doctors had told her that she would likely only live for six months. Yet she went on to live twelve more years after that diagnosis. But when she eventually did pass away, I cried for weeks, and I didn't know how to deal with the awful pain I had in my heart. At the young age of twelve, I couldn't understand why a God, who I didn't really know, but a God that everyone went to church to sing about and hear about, would take one of the people I cared for the most away from me. This was when everything started to spiral downhill quite rapidly.

When my Granna died, everyone on my dad's side of the family was very torn up; dealing with their own pain, so much so, that I believe no one knew how to help me deal with mine. Consequently, a huge wound of resentment began to grow within me. I remember that the night she passed away, I was staying with my other grandparents, Nanny and Papa. They received a phone call from my dad. I don't really believe now that he ever said this, but at the time the enemy got me to believe that my dad lied to me and told me she was doing alright instead of telling me she had passed away. I was so deceived into believing that my dad lied to me that it led me to subconsciously make a vow to never trust anyone again. I didn't realize that I'd made that vow until years later when God would take me through a deep time of healing where He showed this to me in a very clear way.

Around this same time, I also moved to a new school and started making some new friends. A couple of us would become pretty close over the years. I now realize that they were probably not the best to hang around with. Some of them had grown up with alcohol and drugs in their homes all of their whole lives. Some had older brothers who used, and some even had parents who were involved in drugs. These new friends had a bit more of an understanding of that lifestyle than I did. Eventually, my grades started to slip, and in the end, we all started using drugs. I had smoked cigarettes some before this and had been drunk once – so bad that I threw up for two days straight. But when we started using drugs, everything changed. I had no idea what I was getting myself in to. I don't think any of us had much of an idea. Never did I think it would take me down such a dark road as it did.

Chapter 2

THE DOWNWARD SPIRAL

The first drug I ever really remember using, when I was 12 years old, was crystal meth or speed as some people call it. It goes by many names - crystal meth, speed, crank, ice, methamphetamine, and glass are just a few. I may have used other drugs before that, I guess, but this drug took me to a place none of the others did, which is probably why I remember it the most. I remember that moment as if it happened only a few days back even though it was almost 20 years ago. We were in my best friend's room at the time, and he had acquired some of it. I had no idea what it was but, everyone in the room was doing it, so I joined in too. It was unlike anything I'd ever experienced. Instantly I was high and felt like I was a foot taller than I actually was. I started to notice every speck of dirt around me in a very paranoid way and felt like I could go for days without sleep. The next day it wore off, and I was sick as could be. All I wanted to do at that point was sleep for days; yet even though at that moment I felt so sick, I was also so intrigued by the high the crystal meth had given me, that the sickness didn't deter me from trying it again.

It has a very distinct smell and taste, but you'd only know what I'm talking about if you've ever done it yourself. It's dirty, and after using it for some time, you begin to feel gross and unclean. Sometimes after I used the stuff, I felt that I could take a thousand showers and still never feel clean. That makes complete sense once you know what the stuff is made out of. Many of the chemicals that make up speed can be found right under your kitchen sink. Some of which, if ingested by themselves, could kill you.

Speed is one of those drugs that can keep you up for days and days and days without any sleep at all, and it will take away all desire for food as well. I, myself could lose up to 15 pounds in a matter of four or five days if I used enough. In no time at all after continuous use, I would begin to look like walking death. After a lengthy period of using speed and not sleeping, the mind begins to play tricks on you so I would see things that weren't there and also have very demonic hallucinations. It would cause me to have hour-long conversations with people who weren't even there; it put me in such a paranoid place that I often thought someone was trying to kill me. I remember many times I would be so paranoid that I would look out the windows of our house all night long because I was convinced someone was out there in the woods behind our house and they were after me. I remember the trees moving and casting shadows that looked like people, and I often was sure those shadows were people moving around in the yard.

After being saved, I came to refer to the drug as The Devil's Candy. Satan tends to use it in such a way that it literally puts people in a demonically possessed state. It alters the mind and deceives them into believing that the life they are living while high is a better reality. It really is a gateway to the demonic world.

My friends and I had no concept of addiction. We didn't know what it meant to be addicted nor did we know what the term addiction even meant. But, we were in every sense addicted. When we couldn't get our hands on the speed, we would often buy the pharmaceutical grade pills called Adderall from our classmates who were prescribed the drug to treat ADHD. Adderall has an almost identical chemical compound as the speed does and works basically the same way. The only difference between Adderall and speed is that Adderall is prescribed legally whereas speed is a very illegal street drug. The reason Adderall was so easy to obtain was probably because so many students had it prescribed for them. If we wanted, we could easily accumulate a full bottle of it in a week or so, which amounted to about 40-50 pills. All we had to do was trade something they valued, which for most was either music CDs of their favorite artist or band or pokemon cards, which were of substantial value in those days.

Sometimes I would go five to seven days without eating or sleeping. Meanwhile, I still managed to go to school and focus on my work at least some of the time while I was there. However, my grades began to plummet drastically as did my physical appearance and my well-being. In addition to using the speed or pharmaceutical alternatives, I was also smoking marijuana on a daily basis. On weekends and practically any other time it was available, I would often be drinking some sort of alcohol too.

Around this time I also started listening to heavy metal music which only fueled the demons even more. I began to wear nothing but black and at times even had my hair died a variety of interesting colors. The music I was listening to at the time was straight from hell. The lyrics spoke of death, the devil, hatred, killing, destruction and various other things related to the occult, witchcraft or paganism. John 10:10 speaks of the thief who comes to kill, steal, and destroy, and that very thief (satan) had come to kill my spirit, steal my joy, and destroy my life in this time before I ever understood the second part of that scripture where Jesus says that He Himself gives the fullness of life.

I was on a downward spiral that would only continue to plummet deeper and deeper as the years went by. I had no concept of addiction when I first started using drugs, and I didn't know that it would be something that would eventually consume my entire life. All I knew at the time was that it felt good and I liked it. Over the years though I would grow to have a violent hatred for speed and what it did to me both physically and mentally, but no matter how crazy it caused me to be, I couldn't seem to stop using it. The darkness that consumed my life was terrible. I wish no one ever had to experience the perils of such a life.

All throughout my life I've never done anything halfway. And in this period of my life, I always took things to the extreme which had some very drastic consequences. I can look back and see the addictive personality at work even when I was a young kid. I thought I had to have every toy in a collection or every baseball card out there. Whenever something new became a fad, like Beanie Babies or Pokémon cards or baseball cards, I would shift my focus and have to have every one of them possible. It only makes sense to me now that it was that same passion for wanting it all (greed and an addictive personality) that caused me to want as many drugs as I could possibly get.

Thankfully, now I've funneled the desire to have it all towards my relationship with God. Some would call it being a radical Christian, but I only know it as the normal way a Christian should live his life. I'm consumed with Him and can never seem to get enough. But I am getting ahead of my story...

Chapter 3

DEEPER DOWN THE SPIRAL

By the time I was 14 or 15 I was into drugs on a daily basis. I was either using speed, cocaine, marijuana, ADHD meds, ecstasy, pain pills or any combination of any of those that I could get my hands on. Even though I tried every drug under the sun, speed seemed to have the greatest grip on me, and it was the one I was hooked on the most. I could've left any of the other drugs alone, but at this time I was so enthralled with the euphoria I received from speed that I just couldn't manage to put it aside.

I remember times when I was as high as I could possibly be, and my mom would still make me go to church with them. I didn't think much about going to church in that state of mind because honestly, being high had become my normal. For several years my parents weren't even aware I was using drugs at all – or maybe they were but just didn't want to admit it. I was so warped in my understanding of what I thought I needed at this time; which was more drugs, that I would often ask my mom if I could put her money in the offering basket at church. And she allowed me to do it! I was sneaky and would put the small bills on the outside of the wad of cash she would give me and stick the larger ones in my pocket without her seeing. My understanding of right and wrong had shifted dramatically, to the point that I didn't even consider how devious I was being. I just wanted the drugs. I didn't really think much about it at the time, but now, as I look back, I recognize what I was doing as sin. Sin had crept into my life and deceived me into thinking that what I was doing was alright, just like everything else going on in my life at the time.

I began sneaking out at night, and I would spend a good portion of most nights down the street from my parents' house with a girl I went to school with named Audrey. She was a couple years older than me, but she would steal marijuana from her parents, and we would get high together. She eventually became my girlfriend, and we stayed together for about five years. I felt bad because I would eventually pull her deeper into the drug scene and get her addicted to speed as well. We often found ourselves in some pretty bad situations. Once we were pulled over by the cops for speeding right after we had just smoked a joint of marijuana that left the car completely filled with smoke. As the officer came to our window and we rolled it down the smoke billowed out directly in his face. At the time I had a substantial amount of speed in my pocket too. It was enough that if the officer had searched us and found it, we both could've been sentenced to several years in prison. To our surprise, the officer didn't say one word to us about it and let us go with a warning. Or the time we were so drunk and decided to go driving in the rain only to run the truck we were driving, which wasn't even ours, into a propane tank, causing the tank to topple over and roll into a house. We also fought a lot towards the end because the drugs literally consumed us both. Our relationship eventually got so bad that we would steal from each other just to get the next high.

In my mind, I had no understanding of addiction and never saw myself as an addict even though I used daily. I would often justify it by saying I could quit for two or three days here or there and I'd be fine, which meant I wasn't hooked on it at all. That was a lie. My addiction grew so bad that I would steal money from my parents, grandparents, and others in order to keep my habit going.

Many of my friends at the time frequently robbed places or broke into cars in order to score more drugs with the loot they acquired, but I couldn't really bring myself to break into cars like they did or do some of the other things they would do. However, several times I became desperate enough to do what I said I would never do, and I broke into a car when I saw something of value.

I remember one time when I was at my dad's house I stole a pistol out of one of his drawers. I took it to the drug house and traded it for about $500 worth of speed. I didn't care about stealing the gun from my dad. I didn't care about trading it for drugs. I just wanted my fix, and I wanted the next high! Only when the speed was all gone, did I begin to feel bad about what I had done. I felt very bad about this one after I used up all the speed, but until it was all gone at the time, I didn't care. For several years my dad thought he had lost that gun somewhere, but one day I felt convicted about it and knew I had to tell him what had really happened to it.

Eventually, I got to the point that I didn't care who I was hanging with as long as they had drugs or could help me get the drugs I wanted. I started to hang with a group of guys who were in a gang if you could call it that. They all wore blue and called themselves The Crips. There was another group running around who all wore red and called themselves The Bloods. We all lived in a smaller town. I know now that these guys were just playing around, and if many of them had made their way into the big city of Dallas, claiming they were part of such a gang, I believe some real gang members may have eaten them for lunch.

Chapter 4

SEIZURES

My life was in such a constant blur at that time that the events that I am about to describe are somewhat difficult to remember. I was killing myself slowly even though at the time I thought I was having fun. If I didn't have any drugs on hand and couldn't get any for some reason or another, I would often resort to huffing gas or chemicals from around the house. Anything and everything that could slightly give me a high or create a buzz, I tried. Little did I know that this constant drug use was having a severe effect on my brain, or that it would eventually cause violent seizures.

The first time I recall having a seizure I woke up in the hospital with family all around me. They looked very concerned. This may not have been the first time, but it was the first one I have any remembrance of. I would eventually start having several seizures a month.

The seizures progressively became worse as the addiction grew, yet I continued putting more and more drugs into my body. On several occasions, I quit using drugs for a couple of weeks, but each time I would be drawn back to them. Every time I started using again, the addiction seemed to get worse than before.

Over the years it got to the point that I could tell when a seizure was coming before it happened. If you don't know what a seizure is, it's when someone blacks out and falls on the floor or on any object in the way, and then shake violently for an undetermined amount of time. Some people recommend putting a wallet or something in the person's mouth during a seizure if you can, because the risk of them biting off their tongue is quite high. Luckily I still have my tongue! The person has no awareness while it's happening and no recollection afterward.

When the seizures first started, I had no idea they were even happening. When I came out of them, usually someone would be standing over me looking at me with the most terrified look on their face. Sometimes I'd wake up in the hospital. Every time I'd ask whoever was standing over me, "What happened?" They'd say, "You just had a seizure." My reply would be, "No I didn't! I'm just sleepy."

Once I was with my Nanny, Papa and Mom on our way to a summer vacation spot and I had a seizure while we were at a gas station refueling the car. I had just gone into the gas station bathroom to smoke some more speed, and the last thing I remembered before blacking out was opening the bathroom door. They called 911, and the paramedics came. While tending to me, they found a speed pipe in my pocket and told my family that I could be given a lengthy prison sentence for having such a thing. They nicely put it on the ground and crushed it to dispose of the evidence so the police wouldn't find it and charge me with having it in my possession, which I'm very thankful for.

What they didn't find though was about $200 worth of speed I had hidden in one of my jeans pockets. When I came back to consciousness this time, I was lying in a hospital bed. As I came out of it, I saw the most terrified look on Nanny's face. Without even thinking about it I got up out of the hospital bed, went over to the sink, took the bag of speed out of my pocket, turned on the water and dumped it all down the drain. The drug was literally killing me and hurting my family more than I knew. At that point I wanted the addiction to end, but it had its claws dug in me so deep that I didn't know how to get out of its grip. In a few short days (weeks?) I was using again.

Seizures like the one above would happen often, but there was really no rhythm or reason to them, and there was no way to predict when they would come. They got lengthier and stronger also as time went on. For instance, I once had a seizure right before leaving our house to go to the airport. We were going to fly out for a cruise, and I had a seizure and fell on a 5-foot long blacklight lamp I had in my room, crushing the 5-foot blacklight bulb to pieces. I fell through the glass fixture and was cut up pretty badly too. There was no way we could miss that flight, so we left and got on it anyway.

The last seizure I had was probably the worst of them all. It happened a few years later. When I was already out of high school. I was driving to work one morning when I went into it. I hadn't had any speed at all in almost a week, but I had been putting a significantly large amount in my system right before then. I think the fact that I hadn't had any in a while is what caused me to have a severe withdrawal from it and is what spun me off into another seizure. When this one happened, a witness said he was driving behind me when he saw my jeep veer off the road into a side ditch. I then crossed back over the entire road, hit something and became airborne. Eventually, I slammed head-on into a telephone pole. When the medics arrived, they called for CareFlite to take me by helicopter to the nearest hospital, because they thought I might have severe brain damage. They even told my family I could end up in a vegetative state. I didn't have my seatbelt on when

I had the wreck, which actually helped in this case. I am not advocating driving without seat belts at all. I'm just saying that in this particular case it worked in my favor. The motor was crushed into the front seat of the jeep due to the severity of the impact, which should have caused me life-threatening injuries. Instead, the paramedics found me on the outside of the Jeep. They couldn't understand how, apparently, I had been pulled out of the passenger side window. Most frontal collisions would have thrown me forward at impact, but somehow I was pulled through the passenger window – before the major impact – which caused me to walk away with minor scratches.

After being saved, years later, the Lord took me back to this accident and showed me that He had sent an angel to pull me out of the jeep. In fact, what I now know as a "Divine Intervention" took place every time that I should've died and didn't. Divine intervention spared my life many times during this season in my life. In this particular instance, if I hadn't experienced an intervention of a divine nature, my legs would've likely been crushed, causing me to be paralyzed or worse.

I was conscious when they put me in the helicopter, but the only thing I remembered later was looking up and seeing my dad's face and thinking, - *Who is this man? And why is he here?* I didn't even know my own dad, which usually would signify severe brain trauma. After being care flighted and being subjected to the usual emergency protocol at the hospital, my condition improved so rapidly I was released and walked out of the hospital three hours later. My only injuries were very minor scratches and two black eyes. Either I didn't have severe brain damage like the medics said I would, or God miraculously decided to heal me at that moment even though I didn't really know Him at the time. Either is a possibility. All I know is that God has had His hand on my life from the day I was born, and no matter how close to death I came; He never would allow it, because He had a plan for me.

That was the last seizure I ever had, even though I still went back to using. My addiction became worse than it had ever been before.

Chapter 5

THE STREETS

A few years before that last seizure took place I somehow managed to graduate from high school. I was always in some sort of alternative school for troubled kids while in high school. It was either one called BRIDGE or another one called PASS. BRIDGE was for kids who continuously got in trouble at school. This included fighting, drugs, non-compliance with rules or a slew of other things. PASS seemed to be for troubled kids as well, but it was more so for those who had fallen behind in school due to bad grades or for girls who had gotten pregnant.

I was in BRIDGE most of my junior high school years and into high school. Later on, towards the end of high school, I was sent to PASS until I graduated. If it weren't for PASS and one specific teacher named Mrs. Strickler who made it her mission to see me graduate, I probably wouldn't have a high school diploma today. Mrs. Strickler wanted me to graduate more than I wanted to myself. She would often give me quite a bit more attention than the other students. Honestly, I think it was because she saw how much potential I really had. She was also my seventh grade history teacher, and in that class, I made a 102 average. I have no idea how that happened since it seems like 100 would be the highest grade you could score. So, it was probably because of my grades in her seventh grade class that caused her to recognize my potential and give me added help during my high school years. In fact, it's miraculous that I not only graduated but even graduated early.

My high school graduation is a blur. I had spent the whole day before and all that night with a friend getting high. We were at the house of someone I didn't even know. My parents had no idea where I was, and neither did I. Somehow they managed to find me in time to get me to the ceremony. I was still so out of it due to the drugs that it's a wonder I was even able to walk across the stage and get my diploma. We had dinner later that night, but I was still so jacked up on the speed that I could hardly eat. Their oldest son had just graduated from high school which was supposed to be a major moment for us all, but I was able to ruin even that moment. I was honestly just ready for school to be over with and to move on. I didn't seem to make it much of a memorable event for my family.

Over the years my mom and dad had many sleepless nights, and there were times when they didn't know where I was for weeks. Dad later told me that Mom would be so worried about me that she had him drive her around all night some nights, looking for me because she thought she could find me. They prayed for me constantly day and night, and I have no doubt that the accumulation of those prayers was one of the main factors in my sobriety years later. For you moms (and dads) out there who have a son or daughter living a similar lifestyle, don't give up!! Your prayers have the ability to carry them through. I suggest you pray over everything they own. Pray over their bed and their pillows, their car, their book bags, etc. Most of all, pray for the day of their salvation to come quickly! I believe it was continued prayer that changed my life as much as anything else.

I couldn't understand at the time how much my addiction was tearing apart the lives of those closest to me, and I thought that my actions only affected me. I was way wrong about that. That's usually the case with most addicts. They don't have the ability to understand why everyone else is so concerned about them, since it's their choice and their own life that's being affected by their decisions. Once you sober up enough to step back and take a look at it all, it's then that you begin to see the destruction your addiction has really caused. You start to understand the hurt and the pain that everyone else went through because of your decisions, and you suddenly realize that it was actually harder for those closest to you than it was on yourself in many ways. An addict can't clearly see the depths of destruction, the death, the chaos and the turmoil that's happening in their life, but those closest to them are almost forced to take a front row seat and watch the whole thing unfold without being able to do much to help them at all. My mom, my dad and everyone else around me were right there sitting front row center.

I wanted so badly to be clean and sober that sometime after I graduated, I admitted myself to an outpatient rehab where they would have classes twice a week. It included a rehabilitation program we would go through. Most of the other people in the class were there only because they had to come, in order to get their kids back or because it was court appointed that they be there. Only a few were actually there on their own accord. I stuck with it for a while and then slipped up and went back to using drugs pretty heavily again. I just couldn't manage to stay clean and sober.

The year after I graduated from high school my parents left town for a trip. It was the fourth of July, and they left me home by myself with a little bit of money for food. That whole week I had people in and out of their house buying and selling drugs. And as if my drug habit wasn't bad enough, I decided to do what I said I would never do. For the first time that week I went from smoking, snorting and eating speed to using it intravenously through a syringe, which is the quickest way to get it in your bloodstream; it gives you the highest high you can get. I remember the first time using it in a syringe like this, because it put me in a place I'd never been before. It was like my mind was spinning on a merry-go-round for hours and hours. My heart wanted to jump out of my chest.

The feeling I felt within, at that time, I would have to describe as magical. My vision went red; as if I was looking through a red pair of sunglasses, and I thought to myself - *This is it! THIS is the high I've been looking for!* From that day forward, using a syringe was the only way for me. When my parents returned at the end of that week, I still had no food in the house and had spent all their money plus much more on speed. I hadn't slept the whole week nor eaten anything, and at times I was so out of it that I remember walking up and down the main road in front of their house. I was decked out with an arsenal of guns, that I had put together from the gun safe at my dad's house stating that I was on a mission. What that mission was, I have no idea. But I do know that from this point on my addiction would take me down a road even I wasn't prepared for.

After that, things got really bad really quick. Maybe less than a month later, after I hadn't been home for a week or maybe two weeks, I got a phone call. I honestly can't remember if it was my dad or my mom on the phone, but whichever one, I was told, "I need you to come get whatever stuff you have in our house. We're changing the locks on our house tomorrow, and if you don't have it out by then, too bad. Your addiction is tearing us apart. We love you, but we can't take it anymore." Those weren't the *exact* words they used, but it gets the point across. So, I went and picked up what I had at their house, which wasn't much, and eventually traded every bit of it for drugs.

Over the next few months I got so far out there in my addiction, at times I couldn't form normal sentences and frequently had no idea where I even was. I also started running around with a slightly different group of people. This was mainly due to my choice to take my addiction to the next level. Some of these guys were close to 60 years old and had been using speed their entire lives. Some of them were called "cooks" – the name given to those who made the speed or "cooked" it. The younger guys in this new group of "friends" were just as far out there on drugs or even worse than I was. Yet the irony was that there were times when I would get so crazy that even the other users would tell me I needed to slow down, take a break from the drugs for a few days and get some sleep.

I was becoming convinced that I would be an addict till the day I died. The paranoia worsened, the hallucinations intensified, and my physical condition was deteriorating drastically. Whenever people I knew saw me out in public, which wasn't often at all, they couldn't even recognize me. One of my best friends later told me that during this time that I looked like a walking zombie. I was so far out there that I didn't care what happened to me anymore. I often stayed wherever I could, going from house to house, but when I had nowhere else to go, I'd just stay on the streets. There were a few nights I can remember trying to get some sleep on a park bench. I stayed under a bridge once when it was raining. I always thought the cops were after me or that someone I owed money to was going to get me at some point. I was beginning to lose my mind – and quickly.

I don't recall exactly how long I lived on the streets like this. It could've been anywhere between six months and a year. My mind was becoming fried like an egg due to the amount of speed I was doing and the demons I was letting in. We had this thing among the group I was running around with to see who could go without sleep for the most days in a row. I think the longest I ever went without sleep was close to ten days.

I somehow had the ability both to attract people with drugs and to know where I could get drugs. I could get them easily, even when I didn't have any money. They just seemed to find me.

Living house-to-house and on the streets came to an end for me one day. It was after I'd been up for several days and had done way more speed than usual. For some reason, this batch was more potent than normal, causing the hallucinations and paranoia to be drastically worse than ever. Most people can't handle the speed coming straight from the cook because the potency of it is way too high. What usually happens after someone "cooks a batch" is called the cutting process. This involves mixing in a variety of different substances that look like speed. This is done in order to make it 'not as pure' and 'not as potent.' Plus, with this process, the people who are selling it make more money, because by mixing in other substances they increase the amount and have way more of the stuff to sell.

The week leading up to this night I had scored some very freshly cooked speed that was as pure as could be, which was why it was stronger than normal. I was taking as much of the highly pure speed as I could. I walked into my friend's house that day and smelled them cooking speed in the garage. I had been up for many, many days and was severely paranoid. At that point, I completely lost it and began freaking out. They tried to calm me down because they were already running the risk of getting caught since they were cooking it right in the middle of town. After I spent some time freaking out, one of them decided they had to get me as far away from that house as possible. They threw me in the car and took off. I eventually convinced them to drop me off at the gas station nearest to my mom and dad's house. They really didn't want to do that, but I made them do it anyway.

This would be the last time I saw or hung around with any of those guys from that period of my life. I got out of their car, entered the gas station and ordered a hamburger. I could feel what was called a "crash" coming on. A crash happens when someone has been up for a long period of time, and the drugs are wearing off. Because of lack of sleep, their body can shut down and go into sleep mode at any moment. I felt the crash coming on, and I knew that if I put food in my body, it would give me a boost of energy and allow me to keep going.

Chapter 6

CLIMBING OUT OF THE HOLE

The few days prior to this incident, I'd been in and out of paranoia so badly that I contacted my dad's best friend from high school, Tracy. I had been in contact with him to let him know what was going on. We had a pretty close relationship, and at the time, he told me that he would come get me anywhere and anytime I needed him to. As I sat waiting for my food, something inside me said to call my dad. I hadn't talked to my dad in months.

It was an honest plea for help. When he answered the phone, I immediately told him, "Dad, I need help. I can't quit, and I honestly don't know what to do." He said he was going to come and get me. I told him no, that I wasn't quite ready to come home or for him to see me like this.

So, I then called Tracy to come get me, and I stayed in his garage that night. I was way out of my mind that day, but I'm thankful for this man who came and got me and allowed me to stay in his garage until I passed out. My mom and dad showed up at Tracy's house sometime the next day. I had sobered up a little bit, but the paranoia and hallucinations were still pretty strong. My dad and I hadn't seen each other in a long time and for him to see me like this was terrible. I'd seen my mom a few times during this period but never on good terms. I was always high, or I'd call her to come get me because I was so freaked out that I needed to leave where I was, and she would come get me. They genuinely wanted to see their son sober and would have given anything for that to happen. Without my mom and dad it's likely I may not have walked out of that life at that time.

Mom and Dad found a rehab they wanted to send me to in Oklahoma, and I agreed to go. It was a 5-month program where the counselors would run us through these weird classes that were based on a strange religious sect called Scientology. We didn't know it was connected to Scientology at the time because that wasn't advertised up front, or they would've likely found somewhere else to send me. The program cost a pretty penny too, and it took a good chunk of the money my parents had at the time. But they were determined to do whatever they had to do in order to see their son free from the chains of addiction. I didn't know how much it cost at first, to be honest, or I would've never gone through with it.

They came to visit me every weekend or at least every other weekend until I graduated from the program. I was kept so secluded from society during those five months, that after graduating from the program, it was very hard for me to even walk into a gas station and know how to function. I remember the day I graduated. Mom and Dad took me to Wal-Mart, and I didn't even know how to act. There were so many people everywhere that I started to get freaked out. I almost told them to take me back to the rehab so I'd be safe. I knew at that moment it would be quite a process integrating back into society. So, as we made our way back to Texas, I was quite scared. I was riddled with fear at the thought of falling back into the addiction once again and failing everyone around me, especially my parents. I did the only thing I knew to do when we got back and kept myself in their house as much as possible, only going out when it was necessary.

Chapter 7

BACK IN THE HOLE

The rehab had a follow-up program for those who graduated and didn't want to go home because of the temptation they would be faced with to use again. In this program, you would become one of the counselors at the rehab and would be placed in housing with several other counselors. This system was very dangerous because they were placing several addicts who had only been clean for five months or so in the same house. It was a set-up for failure. I thought that this would be best for me since it would put me back in that "safe" environment, so I made the trip back to Oklahoma and became one of their counselors. Within a few months, several of the counselors I worked with were fired because they were found using drugs while working there. My roommate then started to purchase heroin from one of the guys who had been fired and who lived close by.

For a couple weeks I said no when he asked me if Id like to do some of the heroin with him, even though part of me wanted to get high so badly. But then I found out that the guy he was buying from also had some speed, so I bought some from him. I intended only to do the speed, but instead, I mixed it with some of my roommate's heroin as well. This was a very dangerous thing to do. Speed is a drug that takes you in one direction while heroin takes you in the completely opposite direction. For example, speed makes you feel like you're invincible and fills you with an extraordinary amount of adrenaline-like energy where, when taken, you could possibly keep running forever. Heroin, on the other hand, puts you in an altered state opposite of that and often makes you look like you're asleep. After ingesting this potentially lethal combination, I felt like I was going to die. I was so sick the next day, but I had to go to work anyway. While I was there one of the other counselors came in and said, "Mr. Clark, we need to do a random drug test on you today. Today's the day you've been selected." I knew I was going to fail the test before I even took it, but had no choice but to take it.

After getting the results, they said I was to immediately go and pack up my belongings because I could no longer work there since I'd failed the drug test. I then had to call my parents and give them the horrible news of what had happened. They would have to make another trip up to Oklahoma and bring me back to Texas because I couldn't be there anymore. They were devastated, but so was I. I was terrified even at the thought of returning to Weatherford, Texas, because of my history there. I thought there was no way I would stay clean if I went back home. My parents came and picked me up. I was 19 or 20 at this point, and I still didn't have my own car or even a driver's license because of my poor choices over the years.

I'd lost track of my older friends who I'd started using drugs with years back, and when I returned to Texas, all I wanted to do was stay in my parents' house and never leave again. Eventually, I got my license and purchased a small jeep from our neighbors and used it to drive back and forth to work. I'd gotten a job driving a forklift for a company that sold drilling mud to the oilfield. Not the best of jobs, but it was a good starting place for me. That was the same jeep I talked about wrecking earlier in Chapter 4 after having a seizure. I don't very clearly know the order of what all happened next, but somehow I got back into using speed again after running into an old friend at a gas station one night.

I felt so bad in fact that I decided I couldn't live at my parent's house and put them through that again, so I decided to move out. They tried to talk me out of it, but I said I had to go. I ended up staying in Mineral Wells which was about 30 minutes from where I grew up during this time, and what I do remember is that it was the dead of winter. It was cold, but I would often sleep in my jeep, which had no heater. This would only last a couple of weeks because during that time I met a girl named Misty. Misty and I used speed together a couple times, but then she mentioned that she wanted to quit and try to get sober. My thoughts were - All right! Here's someone I can stay sober with! We ended up getting an apartment together back in Weatherford, and we stayed clean for about five months. It was during that time when I wrecked my jeep.

Misty and I got engaged to each other at one point, but she was on the run from the cops for failing a drug test at her probation meeting. One day the probation officer found out where we were living, and she said she had to go turn herself in so that I wouldn't get in trouble too. Misty was placed in a prison facility in Dallas, and Mom and I would go visit her on most weekends. This was a difficult time for me, and I started using again really quickly after she left.

My Grandad (my dad's dad) gave me a car sometime later to help me get back on my feet after wrecking the jeep. The drilling mud company I was working for said I couldn't drive a forklift for them any longer because of my seizures, so I started welding with my dad again. I'd worked for dad off and on over the years. I started hanging out with my old friends again who were like family at the time since we'd known each other forever and a day. At first, they wouldn't let me do any speed because they knew what it would end up doing to me. So instead, I smoked all the weed I could get my hands on and did a little cocaine here and there. I thought that if I stayed off the speed, I would be ok. I must say, I still love these guys to this day and pray for them often. I pray that they too will know the love of God like I've come to know it.

After a time of trying not to do speed, one day I finally gave in. After all, I was putting in my body the drugs I didn't like as much, so why not go and get what I really liked? So, I got back on speed again, and for several months off and on I would even use it while I was working for my dad. I wouldn't show up to work some days and began losing weight rapidly. All the while, I was trying to cover up that I was using again, but I wasn't fooling anyone.

Even though I was frequently getting high again, for some reason, I was still going to church with my family. They'd started going to this new church called New River Fellowship, and I kind of liked it, because the music was a bit more upbeat than other churches I had attended. Most of those churches seemed a bit dead to me, but this one seemed to have life. Getting high was feeling good again, but at the same time, I desperately wanted to quit or die. I'd gotten to the point that I didn't really care about my life. Nothing was going good anymore; my fiancé was in jail, and I was back on the road that I'd tried so hard to stay off of.

The using became an everyday thing again quite quickly. Even though I was trying to maintain a normal life at the same time, I just couldn't keep it up. I remember going to church one Sunday, and some guys asked if I'd be willing to let them pray for me, so I said yes. I didn't know they were going to take me in a room where about 15-20 people were waiting to lay their hands on me and pray, but I let them do it anyway. As they did, I felt something completely new inside me, but I didn't know what it was. This was the day I believe everything began to drastically change for me. What I was feeling inside was the Holy Spirit; the very spirit that raised Jesus from the dead. Even the drugs had never made me feel like this. It was like a high that I knew was good for me, and there was this purity to it unlike the drugs could ever bring. Even though I'd never felt anything like it before and was a bit confused, there was such a sense of peace that I knew everything was going to be alright. It was pure bliss.

Even so, the drugs still had such a hold on me that I couldn't seem to quit using yet. In fact, I used every day the following week and got pretty far out there again from what I remember. Things were changing within me slowly though, and the high just wasn't the same as it once was. I wanted the addiction to come to an end so badly that I was ready to do anything to make it stop.

Chapter 8

CLIMBING OUT OF THE HOLE FOR GOOD

It was either at the end of that week or sometime during the following week that it all began to change for the better; for the worse and for the better all at the same time. It was close to the end of February 2009. I had gone with a guy I knew to pick up some speed in Fort Worth. When we got there, he actually couldn't get it, but he did know how to get hold of some black tar heroin. Black tar heroin is one of the most potent forms of heroin available. So, we went and picked it up.

I knew something was wrong, and that we shouldn't have gone to get it. Actually, I believe it was God trying to stop us. We even had a blowout on my car while we were on the way. The guy who sold it to us was actually nice enough to come to help us change the tire. After that, we crippled back; driving on the donut tire for almost an hour. When we pulled back up to my friend's house in Weatherford, I walked around and went in the back door, so I could go straight to his bedroom instead of walking through the front door and having to talk to his dad. Next, I got a spoon and mixed up the black tar heroin in it so we could then put it in a syringe and use it. I split it in half, putting half in one syringe and half in another. We only did a small amount of what I had purchased, but even before we did it, my friend said it looked too strong. But he went ahead and stuck the needle in his arm anyway.

Within a matter of seconds, he looked at me and said, "Bryson don't do it. I don't know if I'm going to make it. I think that was too much."

I thought for a second but then said to myself that if my best friend was going to die, I was going with him. I wanted my life as an addict to be over anyway, so what better way to go? I went ahead and did mine. Immediately, I sat down in my chair and almost instantly blacked out. He was right; it was way too much for either of us.

What happened next changed my life forever. As I was in this state of overdose, I began to see what I now would call "a vision." I saw myself falling into a pit of darkness. I kept falling and falling, and it kept getting darker and darker and darker. All of a sudden I stopped and was lying in this darkness wondering where the heck I was.

As I was lying there looking around, I couldn't see anything because it was pitch black. All of a sudden, as I looked up, straight above me, the darkness seemed to rip. As it ripped, I could see this brilliant white light shining through it. It ripped a little more, and the light became more intensified. Then immediately, out of the light I noticed something that seemed to move towards me. I couldn't make out at first what it was, but then I realized it was a hand that also seemed to be wrapped in the most beautiful light I'd ever seen. There's a scripture in the Bible that talks about God wrapping Himself in light; its true! He truly does wrap Himself in light! (Psalms 104:2)

That hand reached down and grabbed me. The instant it grabbed me, it was as if I was sucked through the light and back into my physical body. I then became aware that I was lying on the bedroom floor with medics all around me. I instantly had this thought, "**That** was the hand of God, and He just saved my life." My friend was in the living room, also on the verge of death. His brother had been giving him CPR while his dad was doing the same to me until the medics came. When I regained consciousness, there was a little old lady, who happened to be a medic standing over me, looking me in the face she said, "Young man, you're lucky to be alive! We think you could've been legally dead now for a while." I always thought she said legally dead for close to 20 minutes, but I could be wrong about that. My mental capacity, at the time, wasn't functioning too well.

They sent a police unit to come in and search the house for more drugs. They happened to find the end of a pill-case keychain that I used to carry around drugs with some heroin in it. The other end of the keychain was on my key ring with my keys which my parents took off and threw away at the hospital, so the police couldn't trace it directly back to me. I remember them loading me in the ambulance and taking me to the hospital. One of the medics wasn't very happy and kept yelling at me, saying that I was just a dumb kid and had no idea what I was even doing. He was pretty mad that he had to come out and revive someone who had overdosed on heroin.

We got to the hospital, and they placed me in a room where they continued to monitor me. Eventually, several hours later they let me go, but I was still pretty weak from what had taken place. I was so freaked out by what had just happened that I don't think I talked much to anyone for the next day or so.

During this run with drugs, I was also seeing a woman who was a counselor from my Grandad's church who was trying to help me quit using. She was helping quite a bit, but I wasn't giving up so easily. I thought that overdosing was the straw that broke the camel's back, but I was wrong. I almost immediately went back to using drugs, but things were finally about to change.

That next week I continued using speed, even though I'd had such a deep encounter with God. Honestly, I didn't know how to quit and was always under the impression that I'd always be an addict or that it would just take my life one day. When I overdosed, it did take my life, but God gave it back to me again! I was still using, but God never seemed to condemn me during that time. It was His genuine kindness and steadfast love that would help me to eventually step away from it for good.

So, the whole next week I continued to get high. One night I had scored a good bit of speed and was on my way to see the same friend who I'd overdosed on heroin with again at a different place, something was different though. I think this time I was more confused and out of my mind than I'd ever been before in my entire life as an addict. He'd been on probation and at this point was now on the run from the cops. We decided to do some of the speed, and I started getting crazy again like I frequently would when I thought everyone was out to get me.

This friend had likely never stepped foot in a church service and definitely didn't know God. Neither of us really knew God, but after he did some of the speed, the most unexpected thing happened. He sat down on the couch, looked me in the eyes, and said, "Bryson, you need to go back to church. You're much better off when you're in church. This lifestyle is no longer for you. You've got to quit this."

I knew when he said that to me that it wasn't him talking at all, but God speaking through him to reach me. I made my way back to my parents' house sometime the next day. I was so far out there that I thought every vehicle on the road was following me and that the helicopters in the sky were all after me. Everywhere I turned, it seemed like there was a roadblock and I couldn't seem to get where I was going. A 40-minute trip to my mom and dad's house took me over three hours because I kept making random turns to try to evade the cars I thought were following me – even though they weren't following me at all.

Next thing I know I found myself sitting in their driveway. Hours later I was still kind of wondering how I had gotten there. I was so lost and had no idea what to do. All I wanted to do was go into their house and act as if everything had been a dream. I wanted to wake up and for it all to be over. Over the next couple of days, I continued to be quite paranoid. A few nights later I had one of the most powerful encounters with God I've ever had.

Chapter 9

THE EARLY DAYS WITH GOD

I remember it as if it were yesterday. That night I was standing in the living room at my parents' house; the same exact place where for years I had used drugs. And in that same place, God met me. At first, I started to hear this rumbling sound; sort of like thunder, but then it got so intense that it seemed like the walls around me were shaking. Then all of a sudden I heard the audible voice of God, which was a very fearful thing at the time, and He said to me, "My son if I would've allowed you to die, you would've seen what hell truly looks like." This shook me to the core. God had decided to speak to me about the harsh reality of where I was and the fact that if He hadn't saved me, I would have faced an eternal pit of fire. In telling me that, He also revealed that by His grace He hadn't allowed me to die nor had He allowed me to see what Hell looks like. He had truly saved my life, and for the first time, I knew this was the real deal. At that moment my heart was completely broken open. I walked out the front door onto the porch without turning the lights on, the power of God fell on me, and I fell to my knees right there on the porch and out there, in the darkness I met with God. For the first time in my life, my eyes were truly opened, and I began to understand the things I hadn't understood for years. It was almost in an instant that I understood that Jesus' death on the cross was the only way we could ever reconnect with God, the Father. His death was necessary because sin had separated us from God and we needed Jesus; someone perfect and without sin, to come and die on the cross to make a way to get us back to Him. I knew that I couldn't get back there on my own and realized just how much I needed Jesus in my life to make that connection. I somehow also knew that He would give me His spirit and give me a new heart too.

I lay there on my face for hours until the sun came up. All I could do was cry and say, "I'm sorry God. I've denied you my whole life. I'll never deny you again." That night was the night of my salvation; the night I surrendered my life to Him for good. I don't recall the exact date it was, so I've always celebrated it as being March 1st, 2009. When the sun began to rise, I was still there on the porch just enjoying that time with God. It was the most peace I'd felt in my life for years. Everything was still, and I seemed to have this ability to smell, see and hear better. The colors around me were all more vibrant. The sound of the birds chirping was crisper, and the smells seemed to be more distinct. I didn't understand all that had happened at that point, but I knew something was different in me.

I'm not so sure my parents knew how to react to what was happening in me at first. They had seen me say I was done with drugs so many times over the years that I'm not sure if they actually believed it was real this time around. I knew it was different this time though and just had this knowing deep down within me that my life of addiction had finally come to an end.

I started going to church regularly from that point on, and I went to every group meeting I could. I went back to the outpatient rehabilitation groups again as well, which Sue Ann who was the counselor I'd been seeing at my Grandad's church recommended I do. I started reading my Bible, and it was like the words were a refreshing drink of water to me. I couldn't get enough. When I read, it was almost as if the words would leap off the page. After all, it **is** called the Living Word of God!

From that day on God began to speak to me frequently, and I would write down what He said in the journal someone had given me. Sometimes what He said would be for me, and sometimes it was for someone else. I later learned that when I got a word for someone else about their life, it was called a prophecy or a word of knowledge. This prophecy or word of knowledge came when I knew something about someone that I would've never known if God hadn't told me.

I started to pray a lot, but for a long time, I would fall asleep in the middle of my prayers. I would wake up earlier than I had to just so I could spend time with God because I enjoyed it so much. I had my little space in my bedroom with a pillow and a Bible where I would go to meet with Him. Sometimes He would speak; sometimes I would just be still. At times he would give me a list of verses to look up in the Bible and help me understand how they fit together. I just wanted more of Him no matter what it cost me. The new life I had found was worth everything, and I knew I'd never be going back to the old life of addiction again.

I began telling everybody what had happened and how much my life had changed because of Jesus. Everyone I knew had begun to see the change as well. There was no denying that I was no longer the person I once was and that I truly had been given a new life through Christ Jesus.

For weeks upon weeks, I would go to this Bible study with my parents, and would always have these very deep questions about the Bible. People tried their best to answer them, but sometimes I didn't really get a clear cut answer.

The beginning days of walking with God were so precious to me. I loved those days more than life itself. Many times I would have days where I would be in a constant conversation with God for hours; asking Him things and He answering me back. I thought it was what everyone had with Him at first, but later I realized that many people don't hear Him like that. It's not because He doesn't speak to people in this way, it's more because so many people don't believe He speaks like that or have gotten so busy in their daily routines that they fail to listen to His voice. He's always willing to speak, but we aren't always quick to listen.

I always seemed to know that I could have an unlimited amount of God and that the more I got, the more there was available.

At the church, I attended there was a pastor named Pat Kelly who really spoke into my life on many occasions. The sermons he gave seemed to be right in line with what God was doing in me. Our church was in quite a transition and didn't have a senior pastor at the time but decided to hire a man for the position named Scott Crenshaw. His messages often touched my heart in much the same way as Pat's and many of the messages spoken by both of them I can still remember to this day. My life was being forever transformed, and God was using the leaders in my church to speak into me some very clear things that would help me understand with more clarity exactly what was happening in me.

One of the first messages I remember listening to was about the prodigal son. Pastor Scott was speaking one Sunday and chose to use this story for his message. If you don't know the story of the prodigal son, it's about a father who had two sons and lots of riches. His plan was to eventually split his riches— the inheritance – between his sons. However, one son didn't want to wait and asked his father to give him his portion now. He then took his portion of the riches and spent them all on partying and so on. Then when he got so desperate that he was eating with pigs, he decided to go home, hoping his father would at least allow him to be a servant. As he made his journey home, off in the distance, his father was standing on their porch. As he saw his son coming from way off, he began to run to him, and when he got to him, he gave him a great big hug. The son then asked for his father's forgiveness and allow him to become a servant, but the father basically said, "Nonsense!" He then asked his servants to get ready for a feast. He asked for the best robe available and for a ring to put on the son's finger as he welcomed him home.

His older brother had been working all day long in the field and was on his way back to the house when he heard the party taking place. He asked a servant what was happening. When he heard that his brother had returned and they were celebrating it, he wasn't too happy. The older brother was upset because he had always done everything right his entire life while the other brother was foolish and went about on his own way. Then the father told him it was fitting for them to celebrate his brother because he had been as good as dead, and was now alive. He was lost and had now been found. (See Luke 15:12-32)

I realized that this was very clearly in many ways similar to my life. Even though we weren't rich and I didn't have a brother, I was very clearly the prodigal son who had finally found his way home. I was once lost but had now been found. I had died, but now I truly live!

Many of you reading this may be in a similar place or in a place of sheer hopelessness. I'm here to tell you that no matter where you've been or what you've done, nothing is too much for God to give you a new life and welcome you home again. I'm living proof of this, and the hope I found in Him can also be yours. What God has done for me, He can and will do for you too if you will let Him.

I know you might say, "But you don't know what I've done or where I've been." It doesn't matter my friend!

When you surrender your life to Him, it's as if none of that even happened. He will not remember your sins and hold them against you. He's a good father who rejoices in seeing His children return to Him. (See Psalms 103;11-12).

It's called a new life. The old things then pass away, and the new comes! It might have been who I once was, but it's not the me I am today. I'm a new creation through Jesus, and everything truly has changed! (See 2 Corinthians 5:17.)

Anyone who knows me would tell you that my life truly is a miracle. Those who have walked this journey closest to me would say that the drastic level of rapid transformation that's taken place in my life is physical proof that God makes all things new and restores those that are broken back to wholeness.

Chapter 10

THE NEXT STEPS

I continued to read my Bible every day and simply began to believe everything that I read. Some stuff I didn't clearly understand; like raising the dead, but I wanted to, and I knew if they could do it back then in Bible times then I could do it today too! I started noticing a pattern. Anytime God was teaching me something new, the scriptures would almost always line up to that subject just about every time I opened my Bible and read. When He taught me about humility, I would end up reading about humility; when it was healing, I'd end up reading accounts of people being healed; when it was love, it would be love, and when it was faith, I'd read about faith. I didn't know how to find the specific verses on those subjects at first, but He seemed to always guide me to them in His own mysterious way.

One thing I had quite a hard time letting go of was heavy metal music. I had grown quite fond of it over the years. I was almost as encased in it as I was the drugs. Christian music just wasn't the same at all, so I still continued listening to some of my old music for quite a while. God was gracious enough to slowly introduce me to some Christian heavy metal bands that would eventually take the place of the old demonic metal music I was accustomed to for so many years. One day at church, Pastor Scott gave out a challenge to anyone who was holding on to that type of music or any demonic books. He challenged us to consider throwing them in a fire to get rid of them, because if they weren't suitable for us, why would we pass them on to others? So, a couple of us from church got together and built a fire in our fire pit. We began to unload my CD cases little by little, throwing them all in the fire. This was a difficult process for me because I was so attached to many of the bands. But once I got through about 400 CDs, I felt so free that I started burning my old t-shirts and clothes from the past too. I even have pictures of the fire burning the music, and in a couple of those pictures, it literally looks like demons were jumping out of the flames.

God has this way of taking your strongholds and the things that weigh you down the most and flipping them once you surrender your life to Him. He flips them into such a testimony of His ability to save, heal and deliver that it then often becomes a life message that you will carry. This life message can then be used to bring lasting change in the lives of those who cross your path and who are weighed down by a similar struggle.

The struggle is real, but then again, so is the restoration from it. When you allow God to truly access your life in a way that fully gives Him permission to change it all, he will change it. He will come in either like a bulldozer and level it all out quickly, or He will gently step by and begin to take you through the process of clearing out the debris in your life. He's God, we can't really put a limit on Him. He has the ability to restore anyone; at any time, in any way He sees fit. Who are we to say it has to follow a specific formula? We all need different things. God alone knows what each of us has struggled through and what it will take to get us to the place we need to be. Why not let Him guide your path? After all, He is the one who created you!

For years I also smoked cigarettes, and they were one habit I didn't want to give up at the same time that I gave up my addiction. I seemed to think it would be too much to give up at once. Plus, I felt that I needed them some days to cope with the drastic changes that were happening. It was a comfort thing and another addiction at the same time. I wanted to quit pretty bad, but I didn't know how to do it on my own. I knew that if God could take a 10-year speed addiction, as violent as these drugs were, he could easily take away my desire to smoke cigarettes too.

One day I got down to my last cigarette and was determined not to smoke it, but to just keep it for some reason. That night I prayed and asked God to help me overcome the need to smoke like he had with the drugs. I confessed to Him that I couldn't do it on my own and that only He could take it away. That night I was taken into a very profound dream.

In this dream, I was in Noah's Ark, and I was riding a white horse up an incline. As I was riding the horse, he reared back, and I fell off. I was determined to ride him though, so I got back up and tried again. I fell off again and tried to ride him a third time, only to fall off again. After the third time of falling off, I stood up in a frustrated manner and said, "I CAN'T DO THIS!!!!" Then all of a sudden, I turned around to see Jesus standing behind me. He had the same glowing light surrounding Him that the hand of God did when He had rescued me from the darkness I was lying in after overdosing. The light was so bright that I couldn't clearly see His face, but I knew it was Jesus. As I stood there in amazement; almost blinded, because of the brightness shining from His face, He spoke. He said to me, "Do not worry, my son. No matter how hard the endeavor, I will strengthen you."

As I woke up from the dream, the urge to smoke was gone. In fact, I even tried to smoke that last cigarette and made it about 1/4 of the way before I disposed of it. It tasted horrible, and I couldn't even tolerate it. Needless to say, I never smoked again. Just like He took the drugs, He took the need for cigarettes as well.

I knew He was also saying something else in that dream other than just speaking about the cigarettes. I knew He was promising me that no matter what I came up against in my life, with Him; I would always have the strength to accomplish what was needed, whenever it was needed because of Him. That is the same for every one of you reading this. No matter what you face in life, no matter what trial you go through, with Him, you will be able to walk through it all with a success you could never reach on your own.

At one point I even had around 18 piercings in my face and ears. After everything began to drastically change, I took them all out as well, because one day the Lord told me I was using them as a mask so people wouldn't embrace me due to my appearance. As convicted as I was and as much transformation as had already taken place, I knew they had to go. I'm not saying piercings are of the devil or anything like that at all. But for me to become who I needed to be, they had to be put behind me just like everything else. Often times God will ask you to lay down something that's become precious to you in order for you to follow Him more closely, because then at that moment it becomes a sacrifice for you. If He only asked you to lay down things that were easy to lay down, what would you really be giving up for Him? Jesus gave His life for you. You owe Him yours back in return.

Chapter 11

FROM GLORY TO GLORY

At this point, I was learning quite a bit about who I'm actually supposed to be and my true identity as a Son of God. Many layers of lies had to come off for me to be confident enough to live life the way God desired it to be, instead of submitting myself to the lies of the devil. I'd been at New River Fellowship now for a couple years and was growing in my relationship with God and with people quite rapidly. I would often go to the local coffee shop and sit for hours reading my Bible. Several times I ran into a friend who I went to high school with and who had recently started a church with his dad. One of those times he invited me to a New Year's Eve worship event at their church. I had nothing else to do so I went.

While there, I started to feel that this church was exactly what I was looking for. I thought I could grow more there than at the bigger church I was attending. This was a smaller church, but the size of the church doesn't really matter; it's the hunger of the people in the church, honestly. So, I kept going every once in a while to New River which had been a place of huge transformation and deep relationships, a place where the people were genuinely running after God— but I also knew there was something more for me elsewhere for a season. So, I would also go to some of the meetings at my friend's church. Before long though, I had fully made the move to the new church, as I genuinely felt God had given me the grace to make the change.

Taking steps of obedience, even when it causes you to leave behind something that has poured into your life, is hugely necessary. Be careful, though, because there are times the enemy will also try to deceive you into thinking that a move like that is right when it may not be. That's when discernment has to step in. And it's good to have the counsel of people who have walked with God a little longer than you have to help you make those decisions.

So, I made the move to a new church and started getting plugged in. My friend, who was one of the pastors, and I started spending a lot of time together. He listened to and read about these guys from years ago named Smith

Wigglesworth and John G. Lake. Both Wigglesworth and Lake operated in a high level of the healing power of God. They saw people healed everywhere they went and John G. Lake's ministry, at times, would see 200 plus people a day healed. Up to this point, I had thought people and stories like these were fake; I had no faith that healing worked like that today. But now I told God that if I was wrong and it really was Him, that I wanted it. Not long after that a few of us started going out on the streets and praying for people who needed healing.

I remember the first healing I ever saw. We had gone to the hospital in Weatherford and ended up in a room on the third floor. There, we found an older woman who was sitting beside her bed, using a breathing tube. She began to tell us that her lungs were really bad because of the many years she had smoked cigarettes. As we were talking, I felt that I should ask her how she got in the chair she was sitting in. She said that the hospital staff had to place her in the chair since her legs didn't work. We then asked if we could pray for her.

While we were still praying over her legs, she stopped us, got out of the chair, and walked across the room! She looked at us from across the room with tears in her eyes and said, "Thank you. I haven't been able to walk like this in four years." Then, as we were leaving, I felt led to tell her that her lungs were better as well, and she'd be going home in two days. The next day we came back to see her, and she told us, "You're not going to believe this. The doctors said I'm doing so well that they're going to release me in two days!"

After that, we saw people healed quite often, and it is something that I've seemed to carry with me to this day. In one case we came across a man who had a broken bone in his leg while we were at the hospital one day and we prayed over his leg, and the bone was fused back together as if it had never been broken. Doctors took several X-rays of it and couldn't understand what had happened. They even said it didn't look like there was ever a break in it and it seemed to be like a brand new leg bone.

At another time while also in the hospital one of my friends was asked by a woman to come to pray over her boyfriend in ICU who had gangrene in his entire body and was only given a couple hours to live. I remember this account so vividly because of the smell as we stepped into the room. It was a smell like nothing I've ever smelt before or since that day. As we walked in, I smelt the very stench of death. My friend knew though that he had to lay his hands on this man and command the disease to leave his body, so he did just that. Nothing instantly changed, but when we came back the next day this man was sitting up in bed drinking a soda and talking to us. The nurse on call came into the room and said: "I don't know what you guys did yesterday when you were here but 90% of the infection has left his body and we expect the last 10% to be gone by lunchtime."

These are just a couple of the testimonies of healing we saw during these days. Many more miracles transpired during this time, but these are the ones that have always stuck with me most.

Not every person I pray for gets healed, but some do, and that's enough for me to keep praying for every person in need, with the faith that they will all be healed. Jesus healed everyone who came to Him everywhere he went. He then gave us that same power to heal as well. If you want to go deeper in your faith, keep praying for the sick whether you're seeing them healed or not. If you aren't seeing any results, you've got to continue praying. Because if you do, one day it will finally break free and healing will begin to flow through you like a river.

When the church first started nearly 2,000 years ago, it was miraculous. Jesus had gone back to heaven after He died on the cross but told those who were following him that He would send another one to be with them and live in them; the Holy Spirit. The Holy Spirit is His very spirit, the same spirit that raised Jesus from the dead, and He was sending Him to be with us, live in us and give us the same power that He himself carried. When the Holy

Spirit first came, there were 120 men gathered together waiting on what Jesus had promised. They were all praying when suddenly a violent rushing wind came into the room. Instantly they all began to speak in a new language called tongues. Tongues are usually a heavenly language but can sometimes come in the form of a different earthly language as well. This was the evidence that the Holy Spirit had come and had made his home in them.

One night I was in a prayer meeting in the back room at church with two other guys, when all of a sudden I started speaking in this language of tongues. I didn't quite understand what was taking place. One of the guys looked up and said, "Do you know what just happened? You were just filled with the Holy Spirit!" Then I walked into the sanctuary and all of a sudden it felt like an explosion had taken place within me. It was like my whole body was filled with this amazing power!

I left that meeting and went to another meeting the same night. The people in that meeting didn't really understand what I was saying, but I started to tell them exactly what had happened. Then I had this overwhelming urge to pray for a young man who was there. As I laid my hands on him, it was like electricity running through my body, out my fingertips, and into his body. When I finished praying, I was completely drained of energy and felt like my chest was about to explode. I never felt anything like that before, but I remembered reading a passage in the Bible that talked about a woman touching the bottom of Jesus' robe, and that He instantly knew someone had touched Him because He felt the power leave His body. That was exactly what I felt as well.

A few weeks later I was praying, and the Lord told me - *They're going to ask you to be one of the pastors at the church. I need you to say yes.* Two Sundays later the pastor asked me if I'd like to be one of the pastors at the church. I didn't know much about speaking or putting together sermons at this point and still needed to overcome the fear of speaking in front of people, but I had to say yes. I never preached or gave a sermon while I was considered one of the pastors, but I did spend a significant amount of time with people on the streets or visiting with people in the hospital, which ended up being more of a pastoral role than I thought at the time. God was definitely growing me and taking me from one level of His glory to the next!!

This lasted a while, but it would be close to a year before the Lord would move me on to other things. But during that year I was completely transformed and walking at a new level with God. God revealed to me through those men in this church more of who He was than ever before, and He set me on a course to believe for some pretty wild and big things. He spoke some very big promises into my life at this time, and I knew that I needed to believe Him for those promises. Even though I haven't seen many of those happen yet, I still believe, with all my faith, that they will be fulfilled.

New Adventures – New Levels of Glory

This new level of His glory only seemed to increase and increase over the next couple years as I was about to go on one of the greatest adventures with God I've ever had. He would take me all the way across the world to share the message of hope and love He had given me in many nations. As an added bonus, He would give me one of the greatest treasures I've ever had; my wife, Tiffany. Our story is quite an amazing journey of pursuit and love. It is definitely not your everyday sort of story of how two people with completely different backgrounds were brought together. She's never touched drugs nor been severely rebellious as I had previously been. Instead, she was raised as a pastor's kid and was quite structured in her faith from a very young age. However, personality-wise, I'm the introverted type, preferring to stay at home and read a book, whereas Tiff is the extroverted people, people, people-type. Read on, as I share our story.

Chapter 12

TO THE NATIONS

Tiffany is the craziest, most outspoken, and do-whatever-fun-thing-there-is-to-do person I know. She was a hairstylist when we met, and she always had some sort of crazy hairstyle and hair color. She worked for a guy who also ran a young adult's Bible study out of his house, which is where we met, back in 2010. Tiff had a pretty decent career doing hair, but one day the Lord told her she was going to have to give it up for Him. Even though we were on separate journeys at the time, each of us was already learning to live our life continually giving things up for Him. He has always given us something much more spectacular than we had to give up in return.

After the Lord spoke to her about this, she came to

the conclusion that she was supposed to pick up and move to England for six months to do a discipleship school with a ministry called Youth With A Mission (YWAM). YWAM is the biggest mission organization on the planet, with missions based in over 200 countries and with 20,000 plus full-time workers that are all supported by the church. So, she went to England where she did the school and also spent time in several other amazing countries, sharing the love of Jesus. After her school ended, she came back to Texas, never thinking she would go back. About a year or so before, a friend of mine had also mentioned YWAM to me briefly, and it piqued my interest, so I started to look into it myself. When Tiff came back home, she had changed so much that her old friends were a bit harder to hang out with, because they seemed to all be doing the same thing and didn't quite understand how she had changed so much.

We didn't really hang out with each other much before she left, but one day after she got back she messaged me and said she really missed me, and oddly enough, I missed her too even though we didn't know each other very well at the time. We started to hang out occasionally. We began to go to different church groups and did other things together, but we were just friends, or so we thought.

God had a different plan all along though. Everywhere we went, people would ask, "What would your wife like?"

or "How long have you been married?" or something like that. It probably happened 30 to 40 times. Literally, everywhere we went. You'd think God was trying to tell us something, but we were kind of slow at picking it up. Tiff got a call one day from England, asking her to come back and work at one of the upcoming schools, to which she felt God saying yes. She moved back to England six months to the day after returning to Texas. A friend of hers in England had actually told her she would be back in six months and it happened six months to the day! The day before she left, we officially decided to step into a relationship with each other, after understanding that it was God's desire for us to be married eventually.

She committed to staying at least two years in England though, so we both thought we may not see each other until the two years were up. But we were wrong. Shortly after she left, people began giving me large amounts of cash, stating that God said I needed it or that I was going to need it where I was going. They would give random amounts like $200 or $500 or even $1000. It happened quite frequently. So, I accumulated the cash, and eventually, I had enough to do the DISCIPLESHIP school in England myself.

Around that time, one of the women who I consider a spiritual mother to me told me that she was going to start praying that God would send me to England to be with Tiff. Also, in a dream, God gave me a picture of the YWAM base there in England before I'd ever seen it. I asked Tiff to send me a picture of the mission base there, and it was the same picture God had given me in my dream. I knew I was supposed to go, but I hadn't committed to it yet. We both knew we were supposed to be married, yet we didn't quite know when it would happen or how. God has a way of working out the details for you sometimes when all you have to do is give him your yes.

One day at church a friend of mine me about a church in Dallas I should go check out called The Upper Room. They happened to have a 5 pm service that day, so I decided to go check it out. I arrived a bit early, so I sat in the parking lot on the phone with Tiff in England. I told her I was ready to make the commitment to come to England and do a DTS (Discipleship Training School). Thirty minutes later I was sitting in the church service, which happened to have guest speakers that day. The speakers had been traveling throughout Europe as missionaries for 10 years with only two backpacks.

As they were talking, the pastor stood up and said, "Hold everything! I just got this text message that someone here has decided to move to England and I think we need to pray for you." My sister, Kalli, was with me, and she instantly looked over at me with a look that said - *Woah, it's getting real now!* I went up to the front, and they prayed for me. Then the missionaries asked what I was going to be doing in England, so I told them about my plans to go do a discipleship school with YWAM, and where it was in England, and their response was, "We used to work on that exact same YWAM base years ago." If that was not a clear enough confirmation that I should go, then I didn't know what was.

I knew from this point, and it was very clear that I would definitely be meeting my bride-to-be in England but didn't know exactly how soon. She left for England in August of 2013, and by December I had already received all the money I needed. I sold everything I owned and prepared everything for my move to England. At this point in my life, I had never been on any mission trips outside of the US and had briefly done just a couple here inside the US. So, taking a step and moving across the world like this for two years was huge, but this was God's way of getting me out into the nations. He had also confirmed to me that Tiff was to be my wife. Sometimes we have to pursue the promises of God with our whole heart if we desire to truly receive them. Moving to England was my pursuit of this promise and many other promises He had made as well.

On December 3rd I landed in England and by the 8th Tiff, and I were already engaged. I moved quickly because, well, it's not every day that God tells you someone is supposed to be your wife! We started making plans for the wedding and settled on having it in the summer of 2014. The next few months were an interesting time, though – Tiff went to Romania for two months and then two weeks after she got back, I left for Thailand. About three months later, when I finally returned from Thailand, there was only about a month or so until the wedding. I knew very few details about it because I'd been all the way on the other side of the world, and keeping in contact had been hard. God had his hand in every part of it, however. The enemy did try to separate us a couple times during those months, but he wasn't successful. Within an eight-month period we may have seen each other a total of about two months.

During those eight months, we would have some challenging times as a couple, but also some of the best times for me personally, while I was in Thailand. We had a team of around 20 people with us, ministering in several places throughout northern Thailand including Chiang Mai and Mai Sae which is in an area known as the Golden Triangle. It was always interesting to me that God would send me into this area called the Golden Triangle because at one point it was known for being the world's #1 area for production of opium which then gets turned into heroin. With my history and being that I met God for the first time through a heroin overdose, I've always felt like I have some sort of authority over this specific addiction. Over the years no matter where we have gone, there has seemed to always be a door opened to minister to heroin addicts on some level. While we were here in Thailand though I began to see God move in a more powerful way with miracles, signs, and wonders than ever before.

The following excerpts are some of the miracles, signs, and wonders we saw:

Healing of Cancer -

One of the local contacts that we were working within Chiang Mai, Thailand would pick us up once a week and take us to the local hospital. For some reason, we were only allowed to go on one floor which happened to be the women's floor. On the way there, one week, we got behind a car that said MARCH on the back of it in big bold letters. I knew God was saying we needed to MARCH right into that hospital and declare his healing as a "MARCHING ORDER." So, I shared that with the team, and we boldly did that. Several healings took place in that hospital over the weeks; including a woman healed of Stage 4 cancer which was supposed to take her life any day. This was the first healing of a cancer like this I'd ever witnessed. In fact, there were three women healed of stage 4 cancer in the same hospital room. We only laid hands on one of them, but all three received the healing.

Multiplication of Food -

The same guy who took us to the hospitals would take us weekly into a youth prison filled with Buddhist gang members and murderers. On one occasion, beforehand we bought some small bags of chips to hand out, but we only bought 35 bags, thinking about that many guys would come to hear us speak. That was the day I was to share my testimony, and as I shared, more and more of them kept coming. By the time it was over, there were closer to 80-100 Thai guys; most of them covered from head to toe with tattoos, sitting still as could be, listening to my every word. When it came time to hand out the snacks we knew we didn't have enough for everyone, so someone on our team had the idea to pour all the packages into one large bag and just let the guys come get handfuls. By the time it was over, every one of those guys had two huge handfuls of snacks, and we had no idea how, other than to say the food was miraculously multiplied.

The Man on the Street -

Nearing the end of our time in Thailand my friend Jeremy was out doing ministry in the streets; just talking to people. He went up to this Thai guy and began to talk. Jeremy is from Texas too, so he told the man he was from Texas, and then the Thai man asked him, "Oh, do you know where Weatherford, Texas is?" That's my hometown of about 25,000 people! Jeremy told him that his friend (I) was from Weatherford, Texas actually. That man then got out a piece of notebook paper and drew a map of my hometown right there in the streets of Northern Thailand. He wrote down the names of a man and woman and said that they had adopted him and taken care of him when he was a child. When I returned to Weatherford, I brought that map and showed it to my grandad. He said he had known the couple very well; that they had both passed away a few years back, but they had been elders in a local church.

Northern Ireland -

After Thailand I spent two weeks in Northern Ireland, ministering with our team as well. About three months before this, I had been reading a book about Smith Wigglesworth – I mentioned him briefly in a previous chapter. Smith is known for carrying the healing power of God everywhere he went and he would even at times see people miraculously raised from the dead. If you don't know about Smith Wigglesworth, you should read up on his life. I guarantee you it will increase your faith. Anyway, as I was reading about him, I simply asked God to give me the same healing gift that Smith Wigglesworth carried. While we were in Northern Ireland, a man named Brian Jourden from Iris Ministries, which is run by Rolland and Heidi Baker, came to minister to our team and us. In the middle of his message he stopped and said, "I was in a meeting several months ago with Smith Wigglesworth's granddaughter, who was 102 years old. She laid her hands on me and imparted to me the healing gift carried by Smith Wigglesworth. Somebody here has been asking for that gift, and I'm here to impart it to you as well." He had no idea I had asked God for that, and frankly, I had forgotten about that prayer myself until he said that.

God's ways are a mystery sometimes, but the more time we spend with Him in prayer, the better we will understand the way He does things. That connection was made on that day, and as crazy as that story sounds, it was just God confirming the scripture in Mark 11:24 that says, "Therefore whatever you ask in Jesus Name, believe that you have received it and it shall be yours." This is walking by faith; that you would believe that you have received something before you even ever received it, which is being "sure of what you hope for and certain of what you have not yet seen." (Hebrews 11:1)

Across the street from the church where he was ministering to us was a business called "BRYSON FUTURE

SKILLS." I knew that I knew that I knew that God was calling me out by saying that what I had received there that day was a future skill I would learn to fully walk in during my life. Healing came naturally for Wigglesworth. He saw people healed everywhere he went, and it became a part of his life as much as breathing air was. I haven't reached that point yet, but I am pressing on to receive the fullness of it myself!

One Of the First Creative Miracles -

While in Northern Ireland we held an evening service in a church, and afterward we asked if anyone needed prayer. An older gentleman came up and asked if we could pray that his knees would be healed. I put my hands on his knees and prayed. All of a sudden both of his knees started moving as if they were being reconstructed. It was like pieces were moving into their rightful place, and his knees were being made new again. The Bible does say that God makes ALL things new; why not a pair of new knees? After we prayed, he tested out his knees and said, "By George, these knees are new. These aren't the old knees I had for sure. I feel like I'm a teenager again!"

Those are just a few of the miraculous ways God moved during this season. You can see Him move like that too, my friend. I guarantee you of that! After Northern Ireland, we made our way back to England again, and Tiff and I were reconnected for good this time!

Those types of things don't just happen. God's hand is at work in every area of life. He has His hand at work connecting all the dots to your journey, just as He has in mine and Tiffany's. Thailand has become one of our favorite places on earth. We know that one day there will come a time that God asks us to go back to Thailand, and when that day comes, we will gladly leap for joy and prepare to make that move!

Chapter 13

BECOMING ONE

The YWAM missions base there in England was quite spectacular. It happened to be an old orphanage that YWAM had acquired years back and was the perfect place for housing and training missionaries. About 120 people were on the base at all times; living together in a small knit community where everyone knew each other pretty well. When the wedding was getting close, many of our friends gave their time and talents to help prepare for it. A considerable number of family members from both sides flew to England to be there as well. We had a really good friend from Texas who runs a catering business, who even flew out with his wife and catered our wedding for 180 people without charging us anything at all. He even paid for all the food costs. What a blessing that was for us!

We were having an outdoor wedding, but the morning of the wedding it began to rain. (Go figure. It's England; it always rains.) We were asked if we wanted to move it inside since all the chairs were wet, but we said no because we felt that it would dry up, and sure enough, it did. The sun came out and dried everything up, and it was the most beautiful day possible.

We took our honeymoon on an island in Greece, which God miraculously provided for, and it was an amazing time for both of us! Tiff loves the beach, so I decided it would be best to go where we could relax on the beach most of the time. We enjoyed ourselves and were so blessed by everyone who had made that time possible for us.

After Greece, we also came back to Texas where our families had put together a celebration for us. Over 200 people came, and we had two hours to greet and meet all 200+ of them. Many were family and friends. Many we hadn't seen in years, and some that we didn't even know came to meet us because they had heard about the work we were doing overseas and wanted to sow into our lives.

When you're in the will of God, He has a way of providing everything you need to get done what you need to get done. This was one of those times when we greatly saw His provision over our lives financially. Our honeymoon was miraculously paid for down to the penny; we were given just the right amount needed to take with us for food and for sight-seeing. We had more than enough given for us to travel back to Texas, and when we got back to England, we were graciously blessed with abundance as well. We were abundantly blessed all because God saw fit to bless us. We never asked for any of that provision, it just seemed to come exactly when it was needed.

India -

A few months later we took part in running a discipleship school there in England, and through the school we then took a team to serve in India for two months. We initially felt that we would be taking a team of six students into the Himalayan Mountains in the country of Nepal. However, before we had booked our tickets and gotten the necessary visas, the Lord clearly spoke to us about a change of course for the outreach. We were instructed to go into a region of the Himalayas, on the other side of the Nepal border in India.

The First Earthquake -

Three days after arriving in India, I had already made local contact with a man who ran a drug rehab and was meeting with him at the rehab to see how we could help. All a sudden, the whole mountainside began to shake.

Men started running out of the rehab yelling, "Earthquake, earthquake!" Of course, they were yelling in a language I didn't know, but it was obvious what was taking place, so I knew what they were saying. The whole building began to shake violently for about a half a minute or so. Tiffany was on the other side of the mountain with the rest of our team, and neither of us had managed to get cell phone service in India yet. There was no way to contact them to see if they were ok. This wasn't the first earthquake I was in. The year before, in Thailand, we had also been in an earthquake that destroyed some of the most prominent Buddhist statues and temples that had stood for thousands of years. This earthquake happened after we prayed that the idols in that nation would be destroyed.

A couple of days after this earthquake in India, we found out that the epicenter of the earthquake was Katmandu, Nepal, which was right where we had almost decided to take our team. It killed around 20,000 people. If we hadn't listened to the voice of the Lord and changed our course, we could've been right there also. This shows just how important it is that you listen for the voice of the Lord and do what He says. It could've been our lives, yet He spared us in the midst of such a tragedy.

The next two months in India we would see God show up in some amazing ways; through healing, deliverance and the baptism of the Holy Spirit. As we were there in the mountains of India, at any given time, you could hear chanting coming from the Hindu temples strung across the hills. They played it on very loud speakers and broadcast it all throughout the region and city. At one point there was a Hindu festival that lasted nine days, and they would broadcast the chanting from sunrise to past sunset. It was a very demonic sounding worship, and you could actually feel the weight it carried – definitely not the weight of glory. But we prayed and interceded the whole nine days as it was going on.

We trekked the Himalayas, sometimes up to six hours a day, going from village to village; preaching and praying for the sick. Many sick got healed, including a woman who hadn't been able to hear for 14 years.

Deliverance from Demons -

We were reaching the end of one village when our translator said there was one more house he felt we should visit. As we made our way to the house, it took us along a path that was thick with the surrounding jungle. I noticed a fire burning up ahead, which happened to be near the house, and as we came closer, we saw a man sitting under a makeshift roof built out of whatever was available from the jungle. He was burning a fire. We started to talk to him, but our translator said he was speaking some weird language and that he couldn't understand him enough to translate. Then the man led us to the house and took us inside. He began to shake and writhe, almost slithering like a snake at times.

In the house, we met his wife, who our translator could understand. Her eyes were as black as coal, and she was wearing some very strange jewelry around her neck. She began to tell us that she and her daughter would often be scared for their lives because something would overcome her husband at times, and he would chase them around the house with a knife, threatening to kill them. She also said that sometimes he would disappear into the jungle, and they wouldn't see him for days. He would just suddenly show up again a few days later without any clothes. Everyone on our team instantly recognized that this meant he was possessed by a demon. The family was Hindu and didn't know Jesus.

We began to pray and cast the demon out of him. His eyes began to roll back in his head, and his spine began to look like it was going to rip out of his skin. It was definitely the presence of a demon making itself known. But, that evil spirit had to submit to the power of Jesus and leave the man and his family. After about 45 minutes to an hour of us taking authority over the spirit and commanding it to leave, the man's body finally fell to the floor, and the atmosphere around us seemed to be much lighter.

While we prayed, another man and woman showed up at the house and started circling the house chanting the demonic Hindu chants we had often heard through the loudspeakers in the city. They obviously didn't like what we were doing.

As the man's body fell to the ground, his eyes quit rolling back in his head, and he looked up at our translator and began to cry. When he spoke this time, our translator could understand every word he said for the first time. He said that he felt as if there was something new in him and that there was a peace and calmness he had never felt before. He explained that the weight he carried was gone, and then he thanked us for bringing that to him. Another team member then spoke to them about giving their lives to Jesus and told him that what he was feeling was the Holy Spirit. The man and woman both renounced their Hindu gods and gave their lives over to Jesus right then and there.

Only God is able to do such a work. We just had to make ourselves available and step out in faith in order for Him to use us in His work. He can do the same through you. That power is still available for us today; if we will step out and believe that Jesus lives in us through His spirit and that He is the same yesterday, today and forever. Nothing is impossible with God, and all things are possible for him who believes!

In India, we also had our first experience praying for a dead man to be raised. He was our translator's uncle, whom we had prayed for in a hospital several days earlier. On this day, our translator got a call informing him that his uncle had died. Our translator said we needed to go and visit his uncle's house. I didn't know that they were going to bring the man's dead body back to the house and lay him in his bed, but once we were there, that's what happened. Our team was outside the house while the man's family was inside. I wanted so badly to walk right in there and lay my hands on his body and command that he come back to life, but I was a bit timid since I had never faced such a situation and didn't really know what to do. Eventually, a few of us went inside, and we very cautiously touched the man, hoping to see him open his eyes and live again. Our faith wasn't quite there, but we took the step anyway, which in turn seemed to increase our ability to see healing for the rest of our time in India. We only prayed for a couple of minutes, and He wasn't raised from the dead, but I made a vow on that day to never step away from such a situation as quickly as we did this time.

Chapter 14

THE JOURNEY BACK TO TEXAS

While we were in India, we began to see many signs that helped us realized we would be moving back to Texas soon, which meant that our time as missionaries with YWAM would be ending for a while. We will always be "YWAMers," because the years we spent with YWAM were some of the greatest years with God for both of us. We grew more and accomplished more for God in those brief three years than any other time in our lives. It was a deep refining time for us both; where we came to truly understand our identity as God's children and began to better understand Him as our Father. We will forever carry in us the spiritual DNA of Youth With A Mission.

The school was coming to an end. We had finished up the two-month outreach in India and were back in England only for a couple of days when a worship leader named Sean Feucht came to hold a week-long training on the YWAM missions base. During one of his worship times, I very clearly heard the Lord say - *Go over to the side of the stage and look at his guitar case.* As I did, I noticed a bumper sticker on the top of it that said, "THE TIME FOR TEXAS IS NOW." If that wasn't a clear sign for us, I don't know what would've been.

We made the preparations to move back and started the process of closing out all of our financial accounts we had on the YWAM base. There were still a couple of months between the time we made the final decision to move back and the day we actually got on a plane and made the move. Tiff wasn't happy at all about going back, to be honest, but she knew she had to follow me as her husband. We had time to spend with many of our good friends before leaving, and even though we knew it was right, it was still very difficult. We both were going to be leaving a piece of our hearts behind. One day we'll be back in England again. Too many people have told us that our time in England isn't quite finished and that we would be returning again in the future.

We sold or gave away everything we had once again, and took two bags apiece with us as we boarded the plane to move back to Texas. I think my bags had more books in them than anything else. Tiff jokingly told me while I was deciding what to take that I had to have more clothes than books, that's not how it worked out.

We already had a house lined up for us in Texas, and there was a job for me as well. I went back to the same job I had prior to moving to England. The exception this time was that I didn't have my own truck, because I had sold it. This made it a bit more of a challenge, but it all worked out. My hourly pay significantly increased too from what it was years before, even though I still didn't have my own consistent transportation. God's ways are funny sometimes.

Since stepping into missions, it's been my desire to see my own people (Americans) who are called into the mission field take that step of faith and just go. So, when we came back, I was certain that we would eventually be training up people and sending them out to serve in the nations. We haven't yet seen that happen on the level I thought we would at this point, but a few people have gone to the nations since we've been home. Now we are on the verge of believing God for the next steps in our journey with Him. We've been home at this point for a year and a half and are realizing just how much we miss being in a foreign country - somewhere among a different culture.

During this time we have had the opportunity to go to Thailand and spend a month there, however, which was very refreshing for both of us. I also spent six days with a team in the nation of Belize where I was smack dab in the middle of a hurricane with 100 mph and stronger winds, which was crazy.

We had a miscarriage and lost our first child 10 weeks after Tiff got pregnant in March of 2016. This was the absolute hardest thing either of us had ever walked through. Even though that was hard, during that time we also felt God's goodness on a level we never had and got so deep in His presence on one occasion that it was like we were literally in the very center of His heart. Now it's been almost 2 years since we lost our first one, and God has graciously given us another daughter and also a son. Of course, they do not replace the one we lost, but if we would have had the first one, we wouldn't now have our precious Jude Raamiah or Angus Abraham. Jude is an amazing little girl who carries the joy of the Lord everywhere she goes and carries with her name the meaning Thunderous Praise. Angus is one who will be an exceptionally strong father to many nations as the meaning of his name proclaims! We call him Gus, and it may be hard to believe, but he is even more filled with joy than his sister Jude is.

After we miscarried our first pregnancy, the Lord made it very clear to us through several things that it was a baby girl and even gave us a name for her. He gave us the name Eden Elizabeth which means "Delight In The Promises Of The Lord." Even though losing her was hard for us, it has given us the ability to minister to several couples that have also lost babies since that time. If we hadn't walked that path ourselves, we wouldn't have clear understanding regarding how to relate to those who are walking it out themselves. We would never have chosen this but have seen God totally flip it and use it for good.

Being back in Texas has been very tough for us because part of our hearts and many who have become family to us are still on the other side of the world. We know we are meant to serve Him in the nations and believe that one day soon He will send us out to do just that, and once again we will begin going TO THE NATIONS! We don't know how or when but with God, our options are endless, and we hope that as you've read this book, you have begun to see just how powerful and loving He really is!

LAST WORDS

Many of you who just finished reading *From Death to Life* know someone else who could use some hope in their lives too. If you know of someone who could benefit from this book, please consider blessing them with a copy as well. Our goal is to use this story God has graciously allowed us to carry to impact the lives of as many people as possible. We desire to show people the raw and real power of God - to bring transformation and make all things new in the lives of anyone and everyone. If He can do it for me, then He can definitely do it for another! If He can take the life of a man dying from such a deep addiction to drugs and turn that man into a voice that speaks of His goodness and mercy, then He can take anyone from any circumstance and use them in any way He desires! Please share this book with someone who could use a boost of hope!

Blessings,

Bryson Clark

32566559R00066

Made in the USA
Middletown, DE
10 January 2019